Life is like a book

This
Reading Logbook

Belongs To:

_____

_____

Thank you for your purchase!
Please consider leaving a review. We'd love to hear
your honest feedback.

Author ——————————— Genre(s) ———————————

DATE	TITLE	RATING
		★★★★★
		★★★★★
		★★★★★
		★★★★★
		★★★★★
		★★★★★
		★★★★★
		★★★★★
		★★★★★
		★★★★★
		★★★★★
		★★★★★

WHAT TO READ NEXT:

Author ———————————— Genre(s) ————————————

DATE	TITLE	RATING
		★★★★★
		★★★★★
		★★★★★
		★★★★★
		★★★★★
		★★★★★
		★★★★★
		★★★★★
		★★★★★
		★★★★★
		★★★★★
		★★★★★

WHAT TO READ NEXT:

Author ———————— Genre(s) ————————

DATE	TITLE	RATING
		★★★★★
		★★★★★
		★★★★★
		★★★★★
		★★★★★
		★★★★★
		★★★★★
		★★★★★
		★★★★★
		★★★★★
		★★★★★
		★★★★★

WHAT TO READ NEXT:

Author ——————————— Genre(s) ———————————

DATE	TITLE	RATING
		★★★★★
		★★★★★
		★★★★★
		★★★★★
		★★★★★
		★★★★★
		★★★★★
		★★★★★
		★★★★★
		★★★★★
		★★★★★

WHAT TO READ NEXT:

Author ———————————————— Genre(s) ————————

DATE	TITLE	RATING
		★★★★★
		★★★★★
		★★★★★
		★★★★★
		★★★★★
		★★★★★
		★★★★★
		★★★★★
		★★★★★
		★★★★★
		★★★★★
		★★★★★

WHAT TO READ NEXT:

DATE	TITLE	RATING
		★★★★★
		★★★★★
		★★★★★
		★★★★★
		★★★★★
		★★★★★
		★★★★★
		★★★★★
		★★★★★
		★★★★★
		★★★★★
		★★★★★

JHAT TO READ NEXT:

Author ——————— Genre(s) ———————

DATE	TITLE	RATING
		★★★★★
		★★★★★
		★★★★★
		★★★★★
		★★★★★
		★★★★★
		★★★★★
		★★★★★
		★★★★★
		★★★★★
		★★★★★
		★★★★★

WHAT TO READ NEXT:

Author ———————————————— Genre(s) ————————

DATE	TITLE	RATING
		★★★★★
		★★★★★
		★★★★★
		★★★★★
		★★★★★
		★★★★★
		★★★★★
		★★★★★
		★★★★★
		★★★★★
		★★★★★
		★★★★★

WHAT TO READ NEXT:

Author ——————————— Genre(s) ———————————

DATE	TITLE	RATING
		★★★★★
		★★★★★
		★★★★★
		★★★★★
		★★★★★
		★★★★★
		★★★★★
		★★★★★
		★★★★★
		★★★★★
		★★★★★
		★★★★★

WHAT TO READ NEXT:

uthor ———————————— Genre(s) ————————————

DATE	TITLE	RATING
		★★★★★
		★★★★★
		★★★★★
		★★★★★
		★★★★★
		★★★★★
		★★★★★
		★★★★★
		★★★★★
		★★★★★
		★★★★★
		★★★★★

WHAT TO READ NEXT:

Author ———————————— Genre(s) ————————————

DATE	TITLE	RATING
		★★★★★
		★★★★★
		★★★★★
		★★★★★
		★★★★★
		★★★★★
		★★★★★
		★★★★★
		★★★★★
		★★★★★
		★★★★★
		★★★★★

WHAT TO READ NEXT:

Author ———————————— Genre(s) ————————

DATE	TITLE	RATING
		★★★★★
		★★★★★
		★★★★★
		★★★★★
		★★★★★
		★★★★★
		★★★★★
		★★★★★
		★★★★★
		★★★★★
		★★★★★
		★★★★★

WHAT TO READ NEXT:

Author ——————————— Genre(s) ———————————

DATE	TITLE	RATING
		★★★★★
		★★★★★
		★★★★★
		★★★★★
		★★★★★
		★★★★★
		★★★★★
		★★★★★
		★★★★★
		★★★★★
		★★★★★
		★★★★★

WHAT TO READ NEXT:

Author ——————————— Genre(s) ———————————

DATE	TITLE	RATING
		★★★★★
		★★★★★
		★★★★★
		★★★★★
		★★★★★
		★★★★★
		★★★★★
		★★★★★
		★★★★★
		★★★★★
		★★★★★
		★★★★★

WHAT TO READ NEXT:

Author ———————— Genre(s) ————————

DATE	TITLE	RATING
		★★★★★
		★★★★★
		★★★★★
		★★★★★
		★★★★★
		★★★★★
		★★★★★
		★★★★★
		★★★★★
		★★★★★
		★★★★★
		★★★★★

WHAT TO READ NEXT:

Author —————————————————— Genre(s) ——————————

DATE	TITLE	RATING
		★★★★★
		★★★★★
		★★★★★
		★★★★★
		★★★★★
		★★★★★
		★★★★★
		★★★★★
		★★★★★
		★★★★★
		★★★★★
		★★★★★

WHAT TO READ NEXT:

Author ———————————— Genre(s) ————————

DATE	TITLE	RATING
		★★★★★
		★★★★★
		★★★★★
		★★★★★
		★★★★★
		★★★★★
		★★★★★
		★★★★★
		★★★★★
		★★★★★
		★★★★★
		★★★★★

WHAT TO READ NEXT:

Author ———————————— Genre(s) ————————————

DATE	TITLE	RATING
		★★★★★
		★★★★★
		★★★★★
		★★★★★
		★★★★★
		★★★★★
		★★★★★
		★★★★★
		★★★★★
		★★★★★
		★★★★★
		★★★★★

WHAT TO READ NEXT:

Author ———————————— Genre(s) ————————————

DATE	TITLE	RATING
		★★★★★
		★★★★★
		★★★★★
		★★★★★
		★★★★★
		★★★★★
		★★★★★
		★★★★★
		★★★★★
		★★★★★
		★★★★★
		★★★★★

WHAT TO READ NEXT:

Author _____ Genre(s) _____

DATE	TITLE	RATING
		★★★★★
		★★★★★
		★★★★★
		★★★★★
		★★★★★
		★★★★★
		★★★★★
		★★★★★
		★★★★★
		★★★★★
		★★★★★
		★★★★★

WHAT TO READ NEXT:

Author ———————————— Genre(s) ————————————

DATE	TITLE	RATING
		★★★★★
		★★★★★
		★★★★★
		★★★★★
		★★★★★
		★★★★★
		★★★★★
		★★★★★
		★★★★★
		★★★★★
		★★★★★
		★★★★★

WHAT TO READ NEXT:

Author ———————————— Genre(s) ————————————

DATE	TITLE	RATING
		★★★★★
		★★★★★
		★★★★★
		★★★★★
		★★★★★
		★★★★★
		★★★★★
		★★★★★
		★★★★★
		★★★★★
		★★★★★
		★★★★★

WHAT TO READ NEXT:

Author ——————— Genre(s) ———————

DATE	TITLE	RATING
		★★★★★
		★★★★★
		★★★★★
		★★★★★
		★★★★★
		★★★★★
		★★★★★
		★★★★★
		★★★★★
		★★★★★
		★★★★★
		★★★★★

WHAT TO READ NEXT:

Author ———————————— Genre(s) ——————————

DATE	TITLE	RATING
		★★★★★
		★★★★★
		★★★★★
		★★★★★
		★★★★★
		★★★★★
		★★★★★
		★★★★★
		★★★★★
		★★★★★
		★★★★★
		★★★★★

WHAT TO READ NEXT:

Author ——————————————— Genre(s) ———————————

DATE	TITLE	RATING
		★★★★★
		★★★★★
		★★★★★
		★★★★★
		★★★★★
		★★★★★
		★★★★★
		★★★★★
		★★★★★
		★★★★★
		★★★★★
		★★★★★

WHAT TO READ NEXT:

Author ———————————— Genre(s) ————————————

DATE	TITLE	RATING
		★★★★★
		★★★★★
		★★★★★
		★★★★★
		★★★★★
		★★★★★
		★★★★★
		★★★★★
		★★★★★
		★★★★★
		★★★★★
		★★★★★

WHAT TO READ NEXT:

Author ———————— Genre(s) ————————

DATE	TITLE	RATING
		★★★★★
		★★★★★
		★★★★★
		★★★★★
		★★★★★
		★★★★★
		★★★★★
		★★★★★
		★★★★★
		★★★★★
		★★★★★
		★★★★★

WHAT TO READ NEXT:

Author ———————— Genre(s) ————————

DATE	TITLE	RATING
		☆☆☆☆☆
		☆☆☆☆☆
		☆☆☆☆☆
		☆☆☆☆☆
		☆☆☆☆☆
		☆☆☆☆☆
		☆☆☆☆☆
		☆☆☆☆☆
		☆☆☆☆☆
		☆☆☆☆☆
		☆☆☆☆☆
		☆☆☆☆☆

WHAT TO READ NEXT:

Author ———————————————— Genre(s) ————————————

DATE	TITLE	RATING
		★★★★★
		★★★★★
		★★★★★
		★★★★★
		★★★★★
		★★★★★
		★★★★★
		★★★★★
		★★★★★
		★★★★★
		★★★★★
		★★★★★

WHAT TO READ NEXT:

Author ——————————— Genre(s) ———————————

DATE	TITLE	RATING
		★★★★★
		★★★★★
		★★★★★
		★★★★★
		★★★★★
		★★★★★
		★★★★★
		★★★★★
		★★★★★
		★★★★★
		★★★★★
		★★★★★

WHAT TO READ NEXT:

Author ——————————— Genre(s) ———————————

DATE	TITLE	RATING
		★★★★★
		★★★★★
		★★★★★
		★★★★★
		★★★★★
		★★★★★
		★★★★★
		★★★★★
		★★★★★
		★★★★★
		★★★★★
		★★★★★

WHAT TO READ NEXT:

Author ———————————————— Genre(s) ————————————

DATE	TITLE	RATING
		★★★★★
		★★★★★
		★★★★★
		★★★★★
		★★★★★
		★★★★★
		★★★★★
		★★★★★
		★★★★★
		★★★★★
		★★★★★
		★★★★★

WHAT TO READ NEXT:

Author ——————————— Genre(s) ———————————

DATE	TITLE	RATING
		★★★★★
		★★★★★
		★★★★★
		★★★★★
		★★★★★
		★★★★★
		★★★★★
		★★★★★
		★★★★★
		★★★★★
		★★★★★
		★★★★★

WHAT TO READ NEXT:

Author ———————————— Genre(s) ————————————

DATE	TITLE	RATING
		★★★★★
		★★★★★
		★★★★★
		★★★★★
		★★★★★
		★★★★★
		★★★★★
		★★★★★
		★★★★★
		★★★★★
		★★★★★
		★★★★★

WHAT TO READ NEXT:

Author ———————————— Genre(s) ————————

DATE	TITLE	RATING
		★★★★★
		★★★★★
		★★★★★
		★★★★★
		★★★★★
		★★★★★
		★★★★★
		★★★★★
		★★★★★
		★★★★★
		★★★★★
		★★★★★

WHAT TO READ NEXT:

Author ———————— Genre(s) ————————

DATE	TITLE	RATING
		★★★★★
		★★★★★
		★★★★★
		★★★★★
		★★★★★
		★★★★★
		★★★★★
		★★★★★
		★★★★★
		★★★★★
		★★★★★
		★★★★★

WHAT TO READ NEXT:

Author ——————————— Genre(s) ———————————

DATE	TITLE	RATING
		★★★★★
		★★★★★
		★★★★★
		★★★★★
		★★★★★
		★★★★★
		★★★★★
		★★★★★
		★★★★★
		★★★★★
		★★★★★
		★★★★★

WHAT TO READ NEXT:

Author ——————————————— Genre(s) ———————

DATE	TITLE	RATING
		★★★★★
		★★★★★
		★★★★★
		★★★★★
		★★★★★
		★★★★★
		★★★★★
		★★★★★
		★★★★★
		★★★★★
		★★★★★
		★★★★★

WHAT TO READ NEXT:

Author ——————————— Genre(s) ———————

DATE	TITLE	RATING
		★ ★ ★ ★ ★
		★ ★ ★ ★ ★
		★ ★ ★ ★ ★
		★ ★ ★ ★ ★
		★ ★ ★ ★ ★
		★ ★ ★ ★ ★
		★ ★ ★ ★ ★
		★ ★ ★ ★ ★
		★ ★ ★ ★ ★
		★ ★ ★ ★ ★
		★ ★ ★ ★ ★
		★ ★ ★ ★ ★

WHAT TO READ NEXT:

Author —————————————— Genre(s) ——————————————

DATE	TITLE	RATING
		★★★★★
		★★★★★
		★★★★★
		★★★★★
		★★★★★
		★★★★★
		★★★★★
		★★★★★
		★★★★★
		★★★★★
		★★★★★
		★★★★★

WHAT TO READ NEXT:

Author ——————————— Genre(s) ———————————

DATE	TITLE	RATING
		★★★★★
		★★★★★
		★★★★★
		★★★★★
		★★★★★
		★★★★★
		★★★★★
		★★★★★
		★★★★★
		★★★★★
		★★★★★
		★★★★★

WHAT TO READ NEXT:

Author ————————— Genre(s) —————————

DATE	TITLE	RATING
		★★★★★
		★★★★★
		★★★★★
		★★★★★
		★★★★★
		★★★★★
		★★★★★
		★★★★★
		★★★★★
		★★★★★
		★★★★★
		★★★★★

WHAT TO READ NEXT:

Author ———————————— Genre(s) ————————————

DATE	TITLE	RATING
		★★★★★
		★★★★★
		★★★★★
		★★★★★
		★★★★★
		★★★★★
		★★★★★
		★★★★★
		★★★★★
		★★★★★
		★★★★★
		★★★★★

WHAT TO READ NEXT:

Author ——————————————— Genre(s) ———————————————

DATE	TITLE	RATING
		★★★★★
		★★★★★
		★★★★★
		★★★★★
		★★★★★
		★★★★★
		★★★★★
		★★★★★
		★★★★★
		★★★★★
		★★★★★
		★★★★★

WHAT TO READ NEXT:

Author ——————————— Genre(s) ———————————

DATE	TITLE	RATING
		★★★★★
		★★★★★
		★★★★★
		★★★★★
		★★★★★
		★★★★★
		★★★★★
		★★★★★
		★★★★★
		★★★★★
		★★★★★
		★★★★★

WHAT TO READ NEXT:

Author ———————————— Genre(s) ——————————

DATE	TITLE	RATING
		★★★★★
		★★★★★
		★★★★★
		★★★★★
		★★★★★
		★★★★★
		★★★★★
		★★★★★
		★★★★★
		★★★★★
		★★★★★
		★★★★★

WHAT TO READ NEXT:

Author ———————— Genre(s) ————————

DATE	TITLE	RATING
		★★★★★
		★★★★★
		★★★★★
		★★★★★
		★★★★★
		★★★★★
		★★★★★
		★★★★★
		★★★★★
		★★★★★
		★★★★★
		★★★★★

WHAT TO READ NEXT:

thor —————————————————— Genre(s) ——————————

DATE	TITLE	RATING
		★★★★★
		★★★★★
		★★★★★
		★★★★★
		★★★★★
		★★★★★
		★★★★★
		★★★★★
		★★★★★
		★★★★★
		★★★★★
		★★★★★

WHAT TO READ NEXT:

Author _____ Genre(s) _____

DATE	TITLE	RATING
		★★★★★
		★★★★★
		★★★★★
		★★★★★
		★★★★★
		★★★★★
		★★★★★
		★★★★★
		★★★★★
		★★★★★
		★★★★★
		★★★★★

WHAT TO READ NEXT:

DATE	TITLE	RATING
		★★★★★
		★★★★★
		★★★★★
		★★★★★
		★★★★★
		★★★★★
		★★★★★
		★★★★★
		★★★★★
		★★★★★
		★★★★★
		★★★★★

WHAT TO READ NEXT:

Author ——————————— Genre(s) ———————————

DATE	TITLE	RATING
		★★★★★
		★★★★★
		★★★★★
		★★★★★
		★★★★★
		★★★★★
		★★★★★
		★★★★★
		★★★★★
		★★★★★
		★★★★★
		★★★★★

WHAT TO READ NEXT:

Author ———————— Genre(s) ————————

DATE	TITLE	RATING
		★★★★★
		★★★★★
		★★★★★
		★★★★★
		★★★★★
		★★★★★
		★★★★★
		★★★★★
		★★★★★
		★★★★★
		★★★★★
		★★★★★

WHAT TO READ NEXT:

Author ——————————— Genre(s) ——————

DATE	TITLE	RATING
		★★★★★
		★★★★★
		★★★★★
		★★★★★
		★★★★★
		★★★★★
		★★★★★
		★★★★★
		★★★★★
		★★★★★
		★★★★★
		★★★★★

WHAT TO READ NEXT:

uthor ——————————— Genre(s) ———————————

DATE	TITLE	RATING
		★★★★★
		★★★★★
		★★★★★
		★★★★★
		★★★★★
		★★★★★
		★★★★★
		★★★★★
		★★★★★
		★★★★★
		★★★★★
		★★★★★

WHAT TO READ NEXT:

Author ———————————————— Genre(s) ————————————

DATE	TITLE	RATING
		★★★★★
		★★★★★
		★★★★★
		★★★★★
		★★★★★
		★★★★★
		★★★★★
		★★★★★
		★★★★★
		★★★★★
		★★★★★
		★★★★★

WHAT TO READ NEXT:

DATE	TITLE	RATING
		★★★★★
		★★★★★
		★★★★★
		★★★★★
		★★★★★
		★★★★★
		★★★★★
		★★★★★
		★★★★★
		★★★★★
		★★★★★
		★★★★★

WHAT TO READ NEXT:

Author ———————————— Genre(s) ——————————

DATE	TITLE	RATING
		★★★★★
		★★★★★
		★★★★★
		★★★★★
		★★★★★
		★★★★★
		★★★★★
		★★★★★
		★★★★★
		★★★★★
		★★★★★
		★★★★★

WHAT TO READ NEXT:

Author ———————— Genre(s) ————————

DATE	TITLE	RATING
		★★★★★
		★★★★★
		★★★★★
		★★★★★
		★★★★★
		★★★★★
		★★★★★
		★★★★★
		★★★★★
		★★★★★
		★★★★★
		★★★★★

WHAT TO READ NEXT:

Author ———————————— Genre(s) ————————————

DATE	TITLE	RATING
		★★★★★
		★★★★★
		★★★★★
		★★★★★
		★★★★★
		★★★★★
		★★★★★
		★★★★★
		★★★★★
		★★★★★
		★★★★★
		★★★★★

WHAT TO READ NEXT:

Author ———————————— Genre(s) ————————————

DATE	TITLE	RATING
		★★★★★
		★★★★★
		★★★★★
		★★★★★
		★★★★★
		★★★★★
		★★★★★
		★★★★★
		★★★★★
		★★★★★
		★★★★★
		★★★★★

WHAT TO READ NEXT:

Author ——————————— Genre(s) ———————————

DATE	TITLE	RATING
		★★★★★
		★★★★★
		★★★★★
		★★★★★
		★★★★★
		★★★★★
		★★★★★
		★★★★★
		★★★★★
		★★★★★
		★★★★★
		★★★★★

WHAT TO READ NEXT:

Author ———————————— Genre(s) ——————————

DATE	TITLE	RATING
		★★★★★
		★★★★★
		★★★★★
		★★★★★
		★★★★★
		★★★★★
		★★★★★
		★★★★★
		★★★★★
		★★★★★
		★★★★★
		★★★★★

WHAT TO READ NEXT:

Author ——————————— Genre(s) ——————————

DATE	TITLE	RATING
		★★★★★
		★★★★★
		★★★★★
		★★★★★
		★★★★★
		★★★★★
		★★★★★
		★★★★★
		★★★★★
		★★★★★
		★★★★★
		★★★★★

WHAT TO READ NEXT:

Author —————————— Genre(s) ——————————

DATE	TITLE	RATING
		★★★★★
		★★★★★
		★★★★★
		★★★★★
		★★★★★
		★★★★★
		★★★★★
		★★★★★
		★★★★★
		★★★★★
		★★★★★
		★★★★★

WHAT TO READ NEXT:

Author ———————————— Genre(s) ——————————

DATE	TITLE	RATING
		★★★★★
		★★★★★
		★★★★★
		★★★★★
		★★★★★
		★★★★★
		★★★★★
		★★★★★
		★★★★★
		★★★★★
		★★★★★
		★★★★★

WHAT TO READ NEXT:

Author ———————————————— Genre(s) ————————————————

DATE	TITLE	RATING
		★★★★★
		★★★★★
		★★★★★
		★★★★★
		★★★★★
		★★★★★
		★★★★★
		★★★★★
		★★★★★
		★★★★★
		★★★★★
		★★★★★

WHAT TO READ NEXT:

Author ——————————— Genre(s) ———————————

DATE	TITLE	RATING
		★★★★★
		★★★★★
		★★★★★
		★★★★★
		★★★★★
		★★★★★
		★★★★★
		★★★★★
		★★★★★
		★★★★★
		★★★★★
		★★★★★

WHAT TO READ NEXT:

Author ———————————— Genre(s) ————————

DATE	TITLE	RATING
		★★★★★
		★★★★★
		★★★★★
		★★★★★
		★★★★★
		★★★★★
		★★★★★
		★★★★★
		★★★★★
		★★★★★
		★★★★★
		★★★★★

WHAT TO READ NEXT:

Author ———————————— Genre(s) ————————————

DATE	TITLE	RATING
		★★★★★
		★★★★★
		★★★★★
		★★★★★
		★★★★★
		★★★★★
		★★★★★
		★★★★★
		★★★★★
		★★★★★
		★★★★★
		★★★★★

WHAT TO READ NEXT:

Author ——————————— Genre(s) ———————————

DATE	TITLE	RATING
		★★★★★
		★★★★★
		★★★★★
		★★★★★
		★★★★★
		★★★★★
		★★★★★
		★★★★★
		★★★★★
		★★★★★
		★★★★★
		★★★★★

WHAT TO READ NEXT:

Author ———————————— Genre(s) ————————

DATE	TITLE	RATING
		★★★★★
		★★★★★
		★★★★★
		★★★★★
		★★★★★
		★★★★★
		★★★★★
		★★★★★
		★★★★★
		★★★★★
		★★★★★
		★★★★★

WHAT TO READ NEXT:

uthor ——————————————— Genre(s) ———————————

DATE	TITLE	RATING
		★★★★★
		★★★★★
		★★★★★
		★★★★★
		★★★★★
		★★★★★
		★★★★★
		★★★★★
		★★★★★
		★★★★★
		★★★★★
		★★★★★

WHAT TO READ NEXT:

Author ——————————— Genre(s) ———————————

DATE	TITLE	RATING
		★★★★★
		★★★★★
		★★★★★
		★★★★★
		★★★★★
		★★★★★
		★★★★★
		★★★★★
		★★★★★
		★★★★★
		★★★★★
		★★★★★

WHAT TO READ NEXT:

DATE	TITLE	RATING
		★★★★★
		★★★★★
		★★★★★
		★★★★★
		★★★★★
		★★★★★
		★★★★★
		★★★★★
		★★★★★
		★★★★★
		★★★★★
		★★★★★

WHAT TO READ NEXT:

Author ———————————— Genre(s) ————————

DATE	TITLE	RATING
		★★★★★
		★★★★★
		★★★★★
		★★★★★
		★★★★★
		★★★★★
		★★★★★
		★★★★★
		★★★★★
		★★★★★
		★★★★★
		★★★★★

WHAT TO READ NEXT:

DATE	TITLE	RATING
		★★★★★
		★★★★★
		★★★★★
		★★★★★
		★★★★★
		★★★★★
		★★★★★
		★★★★★
		★★★★★
		★★★★★
		★★★★★
		★★★★★

WHAT TO READ NEXT:

Author ———————————— Genre(s) ————————————

DATE	TITLE	RATING
		★★★★★
		★★★★★
		★★★★★
		★★★★★
		★★★★★
		★★★★★
		★★★★★
		★★★★★
		★★★★★
		★★★★★
		★★★★★
		★★★★★

WHAT TO READ NEXT:

DATE	TITLE	RATING
		★★★★★
		★★★★★
		★★★★★
		★★★★★
		★★★★★
		★★★★★
		★★★★★
		★★★★★
		★★★★★
		★★★★★
		★★★★★
		★★★★★

WHAT TO READ NEXT:

Author ———————————————— Genre(s) ————————

DATE	TITLE	RATING
		★★★★★
		★★★★★
		★★★★★
		★★★★★
		★★★★★
		★★★★★
		★★★★★
		★★★★★
		★★★★★
		★★★★★
		★★★★★
		★★★★★

WHAT TO READ NEXT:

Author ——————————————— Genre(s) ———————————————

DATE	TITLE	RATING
		★★★★★
		★★★★★
		★★★★★
		★★★★★
		★★★★★
		★★★★★
		★★★★★
		★★★★★
		★★★★★
		★★★★★
		★★★★★
		★★★★★

WHAT TO READ NEXT:

Author ———————————— Genre(s) ————————

DATE	TITLE	RATING
		★★★★★
		★★★★★
		★★★★★
		★★★★★
		★★★★★
		★★★★★
		★★★★★
		★★★★★
		★★★★★
		★★★★★
		★★★★★
		★★★★★

WHAT TO READ NEXT:

Author ———————————— Genre(s) ————————————

DATE	TITLE	RATING
		★ ★ ★ ★ ★
		★ ★ ★ ★ ★
		★ ★ ★ ★ ★
		★ ★ ★ ★ ★
		★ ★ ★ ★ ★
		★ ★ ★ ★ ★
		★ ★ ★ ★ ★
		★ ★ ★ ★ ★
		★ ★ ★ ★ ★
		★ ★ ★ ★ ★
		★ ★ ★ ★ ★
		★ ★ ★ ★ ★

WHAT TO READ NEXT:

Author ———————— Genre(s) ————

DATE	TITLE	RATING
		★★★★★
		★★★★★
		★★★★★
		★★★★★
		★★★★★
		★★★★★
		★★★★★
		★★★★★
		★★★★★
		★★★★★
		★★★★★
		★★★★★

WHAT TO READ NEXT:

Author ———————————— Genre(s) ————————————

DATE	TITLE	RATING
		★★★★★
		★★★★★
		★★★★★
		★★★★★
		★★★★★
		★★★★★
		★★★★★
		★★★★★
		★★★★★
		★★★★★
		★★★★★
		★★★★★

WHAT TO READ NEXT:

Author ———————————— Genre(s) ————————————

DATE	TITLE	RATING
		★★★★★
		★★★★★
		★★★★★
		★★★★★
		★★★★★
		★★★★★
		★★★★★
		★★★★★
		★★★★★
		★★★★★
		★★★★★
		★★★★★

WHAT TO READ NEXT:

DATE	TITLE	RATING
		★★★★★
		★★★★★
		★★★★★
		★★★★★
		★★★★★
		★★★★★
		★★★★★
		★★★★★
		★★★★★
		★★★★★
		★★★★★
		★★★★★

Author ——————————— Genre(s) ———————————

WHAT TO READ NEXT:

Author ——————————— Genre(s) ———————————

DATE	TITLE	RATING
		★★★★★
		★★★★★
		★★★★★
		★★★★★
		★★★★★
		★★★★★
		★★★★★
		★★★★★
		★★★★★
		★★★★★
		★★★★★
		★★★★★

WHAT TO READ NEXT:

Author —————————— Genre(s) ——————————

DATE	TITLE	RATING
		★★★★★
		★★★★★
		★★★★★
		★★★★★
		★★★★★
		★★★★★
		★★★★★
		★★★★★
		★★★★★
		★★★★★
		★★★★★
		★★★★★

WHAT TO READ NEXT:

Author _____ Genre(s) _____

DATE	TITLE	RATING
		★★★★★
		★★★★★
		★★★★★
		★★★★★
		★★★★★
		★★★★★
		★★★★★
		★★★★★
		★★★★★
		★★★★★
		★★★★★
		★★★★★

WHAT TO READ NEXT:

Author ——————————— Genre(s) ———————————

DATE	TITLE	RATING
		★★★★★
		★★★★★
		★★★★★
		★★★★★
		★★★★★
		★★★★★
		★★★★★
		★★★★★
		★★★★★
		★★★★★
		★★★★★
		★★★★★

WHAT TO READ NEXT:

Author ——————————————— Genre(s) ———————————————

DATE	TITLE	RATING
		★★★★★
		★★★★★
		★★★★★
		★★★★★
		★★★★★
		★★★★★
		★★★★★
		★★★★★
		★★★★★
		★★★★★
		★★★★★
		★★★★★

WHAT TO READ NEXT:

Author ———————————— Genre(s) ————————————

DATE	TITLE	RATING
		☆☆☆☆☆
		☆☆☆☆☆
		☆☆☆☆☆
		☆☆☆☆☆
		☆☆☆☆☆
		☆☆☆☆☆
		☆☆☆☆☆
		☆☆☆☆☆
		☆☆☆☆☆
		☆☆☆☆☆
		☆☆☆☆☆
		☆☆☆☆☆

WHAT TO READ NEXT:

Author ———————— Genre(s) ————————

DATE	TITLE	RATING
		★★★★★
		★★★★★
		★★★★★
		★★★★★
		★★★★★
		★★★★★
		★★★★★
		★★★★★
		★★★★★
		★★★★★
		★★★★★
		★★★★★

WHAT TO READ NEXT:

Author ———————————————— Genre(s) ————————————

DATE	TITLE	RATING
		★★★★★
		★★★★★
		★★★★★
		★★★★★
		★★★★★
		★★★★★
		★★★★★
		★★★★★
		★★★★★
		★★★★★
		★★★★★
		★★★★★

WHAT TO READ NEXT:

Author ———————————— Genre(s) ————————————

DATE	TITLE	RATING
		★★★★★
		★★★★★
		★★★★★
		★★★★★
		★★★★★
		★★★★★
		★★★★★
		★★★★★
		★★★★★
		★★★★★
		★★★★★
		★★★★★

WHAT TO READ NEXT:

Author ————————————— Genre(s) —————————————

DATE	TITLE	RATING
		★★★★★
		★★★★★
		★★★★★
		★★★★★
		★★★★★
		★★★★★
		★★★★★
		★★★★★
		★★★★★
		★★★★★
		★★★★★
		★★★★★

WHAT TO READ NEXT:

Author ———————————— Genre(s) ————————————

DATE	TITLE	RATING
		★★★★★
		★★★★★
		★★★★★
		★★★★★
		★★★★★
		★★★★★
		★★★★★
		★★★★★
		★★★★★
		★★★★★
		★★★★★
		★★★★★

WHAT TO READ NEXT:

Author ———————————— Genre(s) ————————————

DATE	TITLE		RATING
			★★★★★
			★★★★★
			★★★★★
			★★★★★
			★★★★★
			★★★★★
			★★★★★
			★★★★★
			★★★★★
			★★★★★
			★★★★★
			★★★★★

WHAT TO READ NEXT:

Author _____ Genre(s) _____

DATE	TITLE	RATING
		★★★★★
		★★★★★
		★★★★★
		★★★★★
		★★★★★
		★★★★★
		★★★★★
		★★★★★
		★★★★★
		★★★★★
		★★★★★
		★★★★★

WHAT TO READ NEXT:

Author —————————————— Genre(s) ——————————

DATE	TITLE	RATING
		★★★★★
		★★★★★
		★★★★★
		★★★★★
		★★★★★
		★★★★★
		★★★★★
		★★★★★
		★★★★★
		★★★★★
		★★★★★
		★★★★★

WHAT TO READ NEXT:

Author ——————— Genre(s) ———————

DATE	TITLE	RATING
		★★★★
		★★★★
		★★★★
		★★★★
		★★★★
		★★★★
		★★★★
		★★★★
		★★★★
		★★★★
		★★★★
		★★★★

WHAT TO READ NEXT:

...hor ——————————————— Genre(s) ——————

DATE	TITLE	RATING
		★★★★★
		★★★★★
		★★★★★
		★★★★★
		★★★★★
		★★★★★
		★★★★★
		★★★★★
		★★★★★
		★★★★★
		★★★★★
		★★★★★

...HAT TO READ NEXT:

Author ——————————— Genre(s) ——————————

DATE	TITLE	RATING
		★★★★★
		★★★★★
		★★★★★
		★★★★★
		★★★★★
		★★★★★
		★★★★★
		★★★★★
		★★★★★
		★★★★★
		★★★★★
		★★★★★

WHAT TO READ NEXT:

thor ———————————— Genre(s) ——————

DATE	TITLE	RATING
		★★★★★
		★★★★★
		★★★★★
		★★★★★
		★★★★★
		★★★★★
		★★★★★
		★★★★★
		★★★★★
		★★★★★
		★★★★★
		★★★★★

WHAT TO READ NEXT:

Author ———————— Genre(s) ————————

DATE	TITLE	RATING
		★★★★★
		★★★★★
		★★★★★
		★★★★★
		★★★★★
		★★★★★
		★★★★★
		★★★★★
		★★★★★
		★★★★★
		★★★★★
		★★★★★

WHAT TO READ NEXT:

DATE	TITLE	RATING
		★★★★★
		★★★★★
		★★★★★
		★★★★★
		★★★★★
		★★★★★
		★★★★★
		★★★★★
		★★★★★
		★★★★★
		★★★★★
		★★★★★

WHAT TO READ NEXT:

Author ——————————— Genre(s) ———————————

DATE	TITLE		RATING
			★★★★★
			★★★★★
			★★★★★
			★★★★★
			★★★★★
			★★★★★
			★★★★★
			★★★★★
			★★★★★
			★★★★★
			★★★★★
			★★★★★

WHAT TO READ NEXT:

Author ———————————— Genre(s) ————————————

DATE	TITLE	RATING
		★★★★★
		★★★★★
		★★★★★
		★★★★★
		★★★★★
		★★★★★
		★★★★★
		★★★★★
		★★★★★
		★★★★★
		★★★★★
		★★★★★

WHAT TO READ NEXT:

Made in the USA
Middletown, DE
01 October 2023

39878655R00066